# PRAYERS TO ST. ANN

## (WITH NOVENA)

From

Approved Sources

◆

New York
THE PAULIST PRESS
401 West 59th Street

## HOW TO MAKE A NOVENA
## TO ST. ANN

TUESDAY is the day dedicated to St. Ann. A Novena of nine Tuesdays can be made by those who wish to honor her by special devotions or a Novena of nine consecutive days at one's own choice.

In making a Novena recite the Novena Prayers as found in this booklet. If possible hear Mass every day and receive Holy Communion at least once during the Novena.

# PRAYERS TO ST. ANN
## (*With Novena*)

## NOVENA PRAYERS[1]
### First Day

Great St. Ann, engrave indelibly in my heart and in my mind the words which have reclaimed and sanctified so many sinners: "What shall it profit a man to gain the whole world if he lose his own soul?" May this be the principal fruit of these pious exercises by which I will strive to honor thee during this Novena. At thy feet I renew my resolution to invoke thee daily, not only for the success of my temporal affairs and to be preserved from sickness and suffering, but above all, that I may be preserved from all sin, that I may gain the victory over my depraved inclination, and that I may succeed in working out my eternal salvation. O my powerful Protectress, do not let me lose my soul, but obtain for me the grace of winning my way to heaven, there with thee, thy blessed spouse and thy glorious daughter, to sing the praise of the most holy and adorable Trinity forever and ever. Amen.

[1]Novena prayers reprinted by permission from a booklet distributed at shrine of Sainte Anne de Beaupre, Quebec, Canada.

*Practice:* Honor Good St. Ann all the days of your life, by some prayer or short ejaculation.

## Second Day

Glorious St. Ann, how canst thou be otherwise than overflowing with tenderness towards poor sinners like myself, since thou art the grandmother of Him Who shed His Blood for them, and the mother of her whom the saints call the advocate of sinners? To thee, therefore, I address my prayers with confidence. Vouchsafe to commend me to Jesus and Mary so that, at thy request, they may grant me remission of my sins, perseverance, the love of God, charity for all mankind, and the special grace (*name it*) of which I stand in need at this present time. O my powerful Protectress, let me not lose my soul, but obtain for me that, through the merits of Jesus Christ and the intercession of Mary, I may have the happiness of seeing them, of loving and praising them with thee for all eternity. Amen.

*Practice:* When you pray to St. Ann do not fail to ask of her the love of Jesus and

Mary. It is the most beneficial prayer you can offer and it will always be granted.

## Third Day

Beloved of Jesus, Mary and Joseph, Mother of the Queen of Heaven, take us, and all who are dear to us, under thy special care. Obtain for us the virtues thou didst instill into the heart of her who was destined to become the Mother of God, and the graces with which thou wast endowed. Sublime model of Christian womanhood! Pray that we may imitate thy example in our homes and families, listen to our petitions, and obtain our requests. Guardian of the infancy and childhood of the most Blessed Virgin Mary, obtain the graces necessary for all who enter the marriage state, that imitating thy virtues they may sanctify their homes, and lead the souls entrusted to their care to eternal glory. Amen.

*Practice:* Ask of God, through the intercession of St. Ann and of St. Joachim, the virtues proper to your state of life and the grace to worthily fulfill all its obligations.

[5]

## Fourth Day

Glorious Saint, I kneel in confidence at thy feet for thou also hast tasted the bitterness and sorrow of life. My necessities, the cause of my tears, are as follows: (*Name them*). Good St. Ann, thou, who didst suffer much during the twenty years that preceded thy glorious maternity, I beseech thee, by all thy sufferings and humiliations, to grant my prayer. I pray thee, through thy love for thy glorious spouse, through thy love for thy immaculate child, through the joy thou didst feel at the moment of her happy birth, not to refuse me. Bless me, bless my family and all who are dear to me, so that some day we may all be with thee in the glory of heaven for all eternity. Amen.

*Practice:* Patience under suffering is the shortest road to heaven, and a great sign of predestination. When crosses overtake you, ask St. Ann to give you patience and resignation to bear them.

## Fifth Day

Great Saint, how far I am from resembling thee, I so easily give way to impatience and discouragement; and so easily give up praying when God does not at once grant my request. That is why I am so wretched and so poor in virtue. Prayer is the key to all heavenly treasures and I cannot pray, because my weak faith and languid confidence fail me at the slightest delay of divine mercy. O my powerful Protectress, come to my aid, cause my confidence and fervor, supported by the promises of Jesus Christ, to redouble in proportion as the trial to which God in His goodness subjects me is prolonged, that I may thus obtain, like thee, more than I can venture to ask. In future I will remember that I am made for heaven and not for earth, for eternity and not for time; that consequently I must ask, above all, the salvation of my soul which is assured to all who pray properly and who persevere in prayer. Amen.

*Practice:* One of the greatest graces you can ask of God through St. Ann's intercession, is unshaken confidence in the promise made by Jesus to those who pray.

## Sixth Day

Glorious St. Ann, mother of the august Mother of God, I beg thee to obtain, through thy intercession, the pardon of my sins and the assistance I need in my troubles. What can I not hope for if thou deignest to take me under thy protection? The Most High has been pleased to grant the prayers of sinners whenever thou hast been charitable enough to be their advocate.

Humbly prostrate at thy feet, I beg thee to help me in all spiritual and temporal dangers; to guide me in the true path of Christian perfection, and finally, to obtain for me the grace of ending my life with the death of the just, so that I may contemplate face to face thy beloved Jesus and thy daughter Mary, in thy loving companionship throughout eternity. Amen.

*Practice:* Invoke St. Ann's aid whenever God requires you to make a painful and difficult sacrifice; she will make it easier for you.

## Seventh Day

O Good St. Ann, so justly called the mother of the infirm, the cure of those who suffer from disease, look kindly upon the sick for whom I pray; alleviate their sufferings; cause them to sanctify their sufferings by patience and complete submission to the divine will; finally deign to obtain health for them and with it the firm resolution to honor Jesus, Mary and thyself by the faithful performance of duties. But, merciful St. Ann, I ask thee above all, salvation of the soul, rather than bodily health, for I am convinced that this fleeting life is given us solely to assure us a better one. Now, we cannot obtain that better life without the help of God's graces. I earnestly beg them of thee for the sick and for myself, through the merits of Our Lord Jesus Christ, through the intercession of His Immaculate Mother and through thy efficacious and powerful mediation, O glorious St. Ann. Amen.

*Practice:* A sure way of making yourselves dear to St. Ann is to be charitable to your brethren, all of whom are her children. Apply yourselves to relieving their corporal necessities; be zealous for their salvation; never let a day pass without praying for the conversion of sinners and the deliverance of the souls in Purgatory.

## Eighth Day

. Remember, O St. Ann, thou whose name signifieth grace and mercy that never was it known that anyone who fled to thy protection, implored thy help and sought thy intercession, was left unaided. Inspired with this confidence, I fly unto thee, good and kind mother; I take refuge at thy feet and sinful as I am, I venture to appear before thee, groaning under the weight of my sins. O holy Mother of the Immaculate Virgin Mary, despise not my petitions but hear me and grant my prayer. Amen.

*Practice:* Holiness is the highest gift to which a creature can aspire. With the aid of divine grace you can obtain it. God even commands you to strive for it with all your might: for that reason are you a Christian. Make the resolution to do everything in your power to win that treasure. There have been Saints in all condi-

tions of life; why cannot you, with the help
of God, do what they have done?

## Ninth Day

Most holy Mother of the Virgin Mary,
glorious St. Ann, I, a miserable sinner, confiding in thy kindness, choose thee today
as my special advocate. I offer and conse-
crate my person and all my interests to thy
care and maternal solicitude. I purpose to
serve and honor thee all my life for the
love of thy most holy daughter and to do
all in my power to spread devotion to thee.

O my very good Mother and advocate,
deign to accept me as thy servant and to
adopt me as thy child. O glorious Queen,
I beg thee, by the Passion of my most loving Jesus, the Son of Mary, thy most holy
daughter, to assist me in all the necessities
both of my body and my soul. Venerable
Mother, I beg thee to obtain for me the
grace of leading a life perfectly conform-
able in all things to the divine will. I place
my soul in thy hands and in those of thy
kind daughter; I confide it to thee, above
all at the moment, when it will be about

to separate itself from my body in order
that, appearing under thy patronage before
the Supreme Judge, He may find it worthy
of enjoying His divine presence in thy holy
companionship in heaven. Amen.

*Practice:* Pray daily to St. Ann for the
love of Jesus and Mary and for victory
over that evil inclination which is most
hurtful to your soul.

## ROSARY OF ST. ANN

This Rosary consists of the recitation of the following prayers:

1. *In honor of Jesus.*
   *One* Our Father.
   *Five* Hail Marys.

   *After each Hail Mary say:*
   Jesus, Mary and St. Ann, grant the favor I ask.

2. *In honor of Mary.*
   *One* Our Father.
   *Five* Hail Marys.

   *After each Hail Mary say:*
   Jesus, Mary and St. Ann, grant the favor I ask.

3. *In honor of St. Ann.*
   *One* Our Father.
   *Five* Hail Marys.

   *After each Hail Mary say:*
   Jesus, Mary and St. Ann, grant the favor I ask.

## INDULGENCED PRAYER

*300 Days—Once a Day*

With deep and heartfelt veneration I prostrate myself before thee, O glorious St. Ann. Thou art that creation of privilege and predilection, who through thy extraordinary virtues and sanctity wast worthy to receive from God, the supreme grace of giving life to the treasure-house of all graces, blessed among women, Mother of the Word Incarnate, the most holy Virgin Mary. Deign, therefore, O most compassionate Saint, for the sake of this lofty privilege, to receive me into the number of thy true followers, for such I protest I am and desire to remain so long as I may live. Surround me with thy powerful patronage, and obtain for me from God the grace to imitate those virtues with which thou wast so abundantly adorned. Grant that I may know and bitterly lament my sins. Obtain for me a most lively affection for Jesus and Mary, and fidelity and constancy in the practice of the duties of my state. Preserve me from every danger in life, and assist me in the moment of my death, so that, safe in Paradise, I may unite with thee, most blessed Mother, in praising the Word of God made man in the bosom of thy most pure child, the Virgin Mary.

*Our Father, Hail Mary, Glory be to the Father—Five times.*

Good St. Ann, pray for us!
*100 days indulgence.*

Jesus, Mary, Ann.
*100 days indulgence.*

## GENERAL PRAYERS

### Universal Prayer to St. Ann

Glorious and holy queen, whom the heavens admire, whom the saints honor, and the earth reveres, God the Father loves thee as the mother of His beloved daughter; the Son of God loves thee for having given Him a mother from whom He took His life and became Savior of mankind; the Holy Ghost loves thee for having given to Him so beautiful, so worthy, and so perfect a spouse; the angels and the elect honor thee as the mother of their sovereign; the just, the penitent, and the sinner consider thee their powerful advocate before God, for by thy intercession the just hope for an increase of grace, the penitent for their justification, and sinners for the remission of their sins. Be, then, kind and generous, and while we invoke thee here below pray for us in heaven. Use in our favor the great influence thou hast before God, and permit not that those who know thee be lost. Show thyself always the refuge of sinners and the asylum of the guilty, the consolation of the afflicted, and give us the pledge of thy kindness. Defend our cause now and at the hour of our death. This we pray of thee by all the love which thou hast for Our Lord and for His mother, thy daughter, that thus sustained by thy prayers we may one day possess eternal life. Amen.

## Prayer to Obtain Some Special Favor

Glorious St. Ann, filled with compassion for those who invoke thee, with love for those who suffer, heavily laden with the weight of my troubles I cast myself at thy feet and humbly beg of thee to take the present affair which I recommend to thee under thy special protection. Vouchsafe to recommend it to thy daughter, the Blessed Virgin Mary, and lay it before the throne of Jesus, so that He may bring it to a happy issue. Cease not to intercede for me until my request is granted. Above all, obtain for me the grace of one day beholding my God face to face, and with thee and Mary and all the saints, praising and blessing Him through all eternity. Amen.

*Our Father, Hail Mary, Glory be to the Father, etc.*

## Daily Prayer to St. Ann

O blessed Mother St. Ann, comfort of the afflicted and refuge of the dying, I, thy unworthy servant, confiding in thy maternal goodness, choose thee, with St. Joachim and St. Joseph, to be my special patroness at the hour of my death. I humbly ask thee to receive me as thy client, and at that dreadful hour to assist me, that I may die in the grace of God, and be admitted to eternal life. Amen.

## Prayer to the Blessed Virgin In Honor of St. Ann

Hail, full of grace, the Lord is with thee. Thy grace be with me. Blessed art thou among women, and blessed be St. Ann, thy mother, from whom thou didst proceed without stain of sin, O Virgin Mary! Of thee was born Jesus Christ, Son of the living God. Amen.

*100 days indulgence.*

## LITANY IN HONOR OF ST. ANN

*(For Private Devotion)*

Lord, *have mercy on us.*
Christ, *have mercy on us.*
Lord, *have mercy on us.*
Christ, *hear us.*
Christ, *graciously hear us.*
God the Father of Heaven, *have mercy on us.*
God the Son, Redeemer of the world, *have mercy on us.*
God the Holy Ghost, *have mercy on us.*
Holy Trinity one God, *have mercy on us.*

St. Ann, Pray for us,
St. Ann, Mother of the Virgin Mary,
St. Ann, Spouse of St. Joachim,
St. Ann, Ark of Noah,
St. Ann, Ark of the Covenant,
St. Ann, Joy of Angels,
St. Ann, Grace of Patriarchs,
St. Ann, Oracle of Prophets,
St. Ann, Praise of all Saints,
St. Ann, Mirror of Obedience,
St. Ann, Mirror of Patience,
St. Ann, Mirror of Compassion,
St. Ann, Mirror of Devotion,

*Pray For Us*

St. Ann, Mirror of Piety,
St. Ann, Bulwark of the Church,
St. Ann, Deliverer of Captives,
St. Ann, Mother of Widows,
St. Ann, Mother of Virgins,
St. Ann, Mother of the Sick,
St. Ann, Light of the Blind,
St. Ann, Tongue of the Dumb,
St. Ann, Hearing of the Deaf,
St. Ann, Comforter of the Afflicted,
St. Ann, never invoked without an-
swer.

*Pray For Us*

Lamb of God, Who takest away the sins of
the world, *spare us O Lord!*
Lamb of God, Who takest away the sins of
the world, *graciously hear us O Lord!*
Lamb of God, Who takest away the sins of
the world, *have mercy on us!*

*V.* Pray for us St. Ann.
*R.* That we may be made worthy of the
promises of Christ.

### LET US PRAY

O God, Who didst vouchsafe to endow
Blessed St. Ann with grace that she was
found worthy to be the mother of her who

brought forth Thine only-begotten Son, grant in Thy grace, that we who devoutly honor her memory, may through her prayers attain everlasting life, through Jesus Christ Our Lord. Amen.

## Indulgenced Ejaculations

My Jesus, mercy!

*300 days.*

Jesus. meek and humble of heart, make my heart like unto Thine.

*300 days.*

O Mary, conceived without sin, pray for us who have recourse to thee.

*100 days.*

Mother of love, of sorrow and of mercy, pray for us.

*300 days.*

Good St. Ann, pray for us.

*100 days.*

## MASS OF ST. ANN

MOTHER OF THE BLESSED VIRGIN MARY

*(Feast day, July 26th)*

### Introit

Let us rejoice in the Lord, celebrating a festival day in honor of blessed Ann, on whose solemnity the angels rejoice and praise the Son of God. My heart hath uttered a good word; I speak my works to the King.

### Collect

O God, Who wast pleased to confer Thy grace upon blessed Ann, whereby she merited to become the mother of her who brought forth Thine only-begotten Son; mercifully grant that, in like manner as we celebrate her solemnity, so we may be aided by her patronage.

### Epistle

Who shall find a valiant woman? Far and from the uttermost coasts is the price of her. The heart of her husband

[ 22 ]

trusteth in her, and he shall have no need of spoils. She will render him good and not evil all the days of her life. She hath sought wool and flax, and hath wrought by the counsel of her hands. She is like the merchant's ship, she bringeth her bread from afar; and she hath risen in the night, and given a prey to her household, and victuals to her maidens; she hath considered a field and bought it; with the fruit of her hands she hath planted a vineyard. She hath girded her loins with strength, and hath strengthened her arm. She hath tasted and seen that her traffic is good; her lamp shall not be put out in the night. She hath put out her hand to strong things, and her fingers have taken hold of the spindle. She hath opened her hand to the needy, and stretched out her hands to the poor. She shall not fear for her house in the cold of snow; for all her domestics are clothed with double garments. She hath made for herself clothing of tapestry; fine linen and purple is her covering. Her husband is honorable in the gates, when he sitteth among the senators of the land. She made fine linen and sold it, and delivered a girdle to the Chanaanite.

Strength and beauty are her clothing: and she shall laugh in the latter day.

She hath opened her mouth to wisdom and the law of clemency is on her tongue; she hath looked well to the paths of her house, and hath not eaten her bread idle. Her children rose up, and called her blessed; her husband, and he praised her. Many daughters have gathered together riches; thou hast surpassed them all. Favor is deceitful, and beauty is vain; the woman that feareth the Lord, she shall be praised. Give her of the fruit of her hands; and let her works praise her in the gates. (Prov. xxxi. 10-31.)

## Gradual

Thou hast loved justice, and hated iniquity. Therefore God, thy God, hath anointed thee with the oil of gladness. Alleluia, Alleluia. Grace is poured abroad in thy lips; therefore hath God blessed thee forever. Alleluia.

## Gospel

At that time, Jesus spoke this parable to His disciples: The kingdom of heaven is like unto a treasure hidden in a field; which a man having found, hid it, and for joy thereof goeth, and selleth all that he hath, and buyeth that field. Again, the kingdom of heaven is like to a merchant seeking good pearls. Who, when he had found one pearl of great price, went his way, and sold all that he had, and bought it. Again, the kingdom of heaven is like to a net cast into the sea, and gathering together of all kinds of fishes; which, when it was filled, they drew out, and sitting by the shore, they chose out the good into vessels, but the bad they cast forth. So shall it be at the end of the world. The angels shall go out, and shall separate the wicked from among the just, and shall cast them into the furnace of fire; there shall be weeping and gnashing of teeth. Have ye understood all these things? They say to Him, yes. He said unto them; therefore every scribe instructed in the kingdom of heaven is like to a man who is a householder who bringeth forth out of his treasure new things and old.

## Offertory

The daughters of kings in thy honor; the queen stood on thy right hand, in gilded clothing surrounded with variety.

## Secret

Look down propitiously upon this sacrifice, O Lord, we beseech Thee, that by the intercession of blessed Ann, who was the mother of her who brought forth Thy Son, Our Lord Jesus Christ, it may be profitable to our devotion and salvation.

## Communion

Grace is poured abroad in thy lips: therefore hath God blessed thee forever, and for ages of ages.

## Post Communion

Being nourished with Thy heavenly sacraments, we beseech Thee, O Lord Our God, that by the intercession of blessed Ann, who Thou wert pleased should be the mother of her who brought forth Thy Son, we may deserve to attain eternal salvation.

## DEVOTION TO ST. ANN

St. Ann is the traditional name of the mother of the Blessed Virgin Mary. All our information concerning the names and lives of St. Joachim and St. Ann, the parents of Mary, is derived from the apocryphal[2] literature. From these we learn that Ann and Joachim had reached old age and still remained childless. Their prayers were answered and an angel of the Lord announced to Ann that the fruit of her womb would be blessed by all the world.

Some writers tell us that Joachim and Ann died before their daughter, the Blessed Virgin, had been affianced to Joseph.

Devotion to St. Ann, popular from an early date in the East, began in the West at Douai and spread rapidly through the Church after 1584.

Tradition tells us that the body of St. Ann was carried to Gaul by the same vessel which brought there Lazarus and his sisters, who were banished from Palestine in hatred of the Faith in the first century of the Christian era. Her precious remains were taken for safe keeping to the city of

2Apocryphal—writings of doubtful authority.

Apt, where the body of St. Ann was buried in an underground church or crypt. The Martyrology of Apt, one of the most ancient in existence, mentions this fact. During the persecutions and barbarian invasions of the time the first Bishop of Apt, St. Auspicius, made special efforts to guard the holy deposit from desecration. The body was buried still deeper in the subterranean chapel and the approach to it carefully concealed.

Peace and security returned to the land with the decisive victory of Charlemagne over the Saracens. At once the people thought of rebuilding and restoring the holy places destroyed or desecrated by the invaders, including the Cathedral of Apt.

The Bollandists tell us that Charlemagne on his arrival at Apt had the Cathedral reconsecrated by Archbishop Turpin. This took place at Easter time. The one cause of sadness amid so much rejoicing was that every effort to find the remains of St. Ann had proved fruitless. A miracle related by Charlemagne in a letter to Pope Adrian I. led to the discovery of her resting place.

Among the young nobles who accompanied their parents on this occasion was a lad of fourteen, John, born deaf, dumb and blind, son of the Baron of Casanova. During the services he seemed to be listening with rapt and upturned face to voices from above. Presently he moved toward the high altar, struck with his staff the steps leading up to it, and made signs that they should dig there. His persistence caused no little disturbance amid the solemn rites; but neither the clergy nor the royal guards could quiet or restrain the youth. Charlemagne, deeply impressed by what he saw, commanded that after Mass they should make the excavation the boy desired. The altar steps were removed and a door discovered blocked with huge stones. No sooner had this door been opened, and the flight of steps leading down from it been disclosed, than the blind boy rushed forward as if his eyes were suddenly opened, and led the way into this underground church. The boy made signs that they must search further and struck the wall of the crypt, indicating that what they sought lay behind this. On breaking down the wall, another and lower crypt was discovered at the end of a long and narrow corridor. There, a bright light flashed upon the king and those present. They beheld a burning lamp placed in front of a walled recess, which flooded the place with unearthly splendor. No sooner had Charlemagne and the others entered this place than the lamp went out. At that very moment the blind boy was given to see, hear and speak. "The body of St. Ann, Mother of the Virgin Mary, Mother of God, is in yonder recess," were the first words he uttered.

The walled recess was opened. A sweet fragrance filled the air. A casket of cypress-wood was discovered containing the body of the Saint. On the casket was an inscription saying: "Here lies the body of the Blessed Ann, Mother of the Virgin Mary."

Charlemagne, after venerating with all present the sacred deposit, had an exact narrative of the discovery drawn up and a copy sent to the Pope. This letter and the Pope's answer are still extant.

## HYMNS TO ST. ANN

### To Kneel at Thy Altar

Of old when our fathers touch'd Canada's
    shore,
They named thee its Patron and Saint
    evermore.

#### CHORUS

To kneel at thine altar, in faith we draw
    near,
Led onward by Mary, thy daughter so
    dear,
O Good St. Ann, we call on thy name,
Thy praises loud thy children proclaim.

To all who invoke thee thou lendest an
    ear,
Thou soothest the sorrows of all who draw
    near. *Chorus.*

St. Ann, we implore thee to list to our
    pray'r,
In time of temptation, take us in thy
    care. *Chorus.*

In this life obtain for us that which is
    best,
And bring us at length to our heavenly
    rest. *Chorus.*

## O Lady High in Glory Raised

What we had lost in hapless Eve,
   Thy Virgin Child restores,
Opening to us in Christ anew,
   The everlasting doors.

### Chorus

O lady high in glory raised,
   Whose daughter ever blest,
The sovereign of the skies hath **laid**
   On her maternal breast.

O gain celestial light and grace,
   Dear heir of endless fame,
For us and all who memory keep
   Of thy immortal name.
               *Chorus.*

To Him, the Savior of the world,
   Whom Ann's daughter bore,
Be with the Sire and Paraclete
   All glory evermore.
               *Chorus.*

# PRAYER BOOK SERIES
# PAULIST PAMPHLETS

## Vest Pocket Size - - -

BOOK OF LITANIES
DAILY THOUGHTS FROM THE LITTLE FLOWER
NOVENA TO CHRIST THE KING
NOVENA TO THE INFANT JESUS
NOVENA TO THE SACRED HEART
PRAYERS FOR THE DEAD
PRAYERS TO THE BLESSED SACRAMENT
PRAYERS TO THE SACRED HEART
PRAYERS TO THE BLESSED VIRGIN MARY
PRAYERS TO SAINT ANN
PRAYERS TO SAINT ANTHONY
PRAYERS TO SAINT JOSEPH
ORDINARY OF THE MASS
LITTLE CANTICLES OF LOVE
NOVENA TO SAINT JOHN BOSCO
SELECTED PRAYERS FOR LENT
STATIONS OF THE CROSS FOR CHILDREN (Illustrated)
STATIONS OF THE CROSS (Illustrated)

*All from approved sources*

5c, $3.50 the 100, $30.00 the 1,000
*(Carriage Extra)*

Individual Package, $1.00 postpaid.

## THE PAULIST PRESS
401 West 59th Street, New York

Excellent Pamphlets
for Bookracks - -

Lightning Source UK Ltd.
Milton Keynes UK
UKHW022210080822
407033UK00009B/118

9 781013 550270